The U.S. Flag

Introducing Primary Sources

by Kathryn Clay

CAPSTONE PRESS
a capstone imprint

Little Explorer is published by Capstone Press,
1710 Roe Crest Drive, North Mankato, Minnesota 56003
www.mycapstone.com

The name of the Smithsonian Institution and the sunburst logo are registered trademarks of the
Smithsonian Institution. For more information, please visit www.si.edu.

Library of Congress Cataloging-in-Publication Data
Clay, Kathryn.
The U.S. flag : introducing primary sources / by Kathryn Clay.
pages cm. — (Smithsonian little explorer. Introducing primary sources)
Summary: "Introduces young readers to primary sources related to the U.S. flag"— Provided
by publisher.
Audience: Grades K-3.
ISBN 978-1-4914-8222-3 (library binding)
ISBN 978-1-4914-8606-1 (paperback)
ISBN 978-1-4914-8612-2 (eBook PDF)
1. Flags—United States—Juvenile literature. I. Title.
CR113.C67 2016
929.9'20973—dc23   2015028504

Editorial Credits
Michelle Hasselius, editor; Richard Parker, designer; Wanda Winch, media researcher;
Steve Walker, production specialist

Our very special thanks to Jennifer L. Jones, Chair, Armed Forces Division at the National Museum
of American History, Kenneth E. Behring Center, Smithsonian, for her curatorial review. Capstone
would also like to thank Kealy Gordan, Product Development Manager, and the following at
Smithsonian Enterprises: Ellen Nanney, Licensing Manager; Brigid Ferraro, Vice President, Education
and Consumer Products; Carol LeBlanc, Senior Vice President, Education and Consumer Products.

Photo Credits
Alamy: GL Archive, 7 (bottom); AP Images, 25; Bridgeman Images: Look and Learn/Private
Collection/Dan Escott, 9; Courtesy of Army Art Collection, U.S. Army Center of Military History,
7 (top); Dreamstime: Ken Backer, 16 (top); Granger, NYC, 11; Library of Congress: Prints and
Photographs Division, 8 (right), 12, 13, 15, 18, 19, 21, 23 (right); National Archives and Records
Administration, 4, 8 (left), 29; ©Peabody Essex Museum, Salem, MA, photo by Mark Sexton, 20;
Photo by the North Carolina Museum of History, 17 (top), 28; Shutterstock: Adam Parent, 26, Arevik,
paper design, Brandon Seidel, 27, Johann Helgason, 5, Joseph Sohm, 23 (left), StillFX, cover, tab62, 17
(bottom), Yuriy Boyko, 6; Smithsonian Institution: National Museum of American History, 22 (right);
Todd Andrlik, author of Reporting the Revolutionary War (Sourcebooks, 2012), beforehistory.com,
14; U.S. Navy Media Content Services, 24; The Walters Art Museum, Baltimore, 22 (left); Wikimedia:
DevinCook, 10, 16 (bottom)

Printed in the United States of America in North Mankato, Minnesota.
009221CGS16

Table of Contents

Primary Sources

What is a primary source? People are curious about the past. They want to know why events happened. People can learn about the past through primary sources. Primary sources are created at the time of the event. Letters, statues, and photos are all primary sources. These objects serve as evidence of past events or places.

a painting of the first U.S. flag raised at Independence Hall in Philadelphia, Pennsylvania

The U.S. flag is a primary source. It stands for freedom and liberty. Other primary sources include the Liberty Bell and the U.S. Constitution.

The U.S. Flag at a Glance

- also known as Old Glory, the Stars and Stripes, the Star-Spangled Banner, and the American flag

- first use of the official flag was in 1777

- has 50 white stars on top of a blue square and 13 red and white stripes

- Flag Day is on June 14 every year.

The Grand Union

The first U.S. flag was called the Grand Union or the Continental flag. Its colors were red, white, and blue. The Grand Union did not have stars in the corner. Instead it had a small British flag, called a Union Jack.

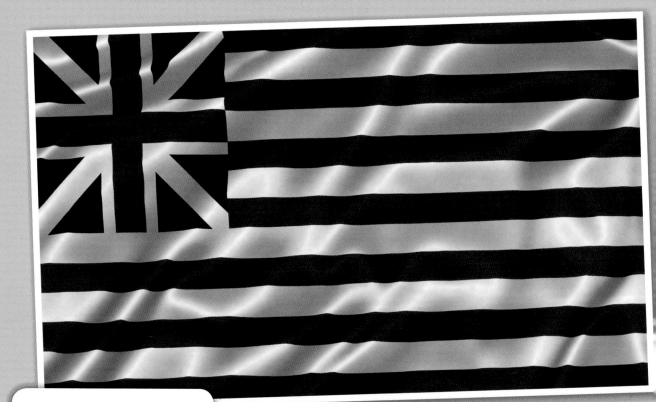

the Grand Union flag

This painting shows the Battle of Yorktown, the last battle of the Revolutionary War.

John Paul Jones first raised the Grand Union flag on December 3, 1775. The flag flew from the Navy ship *Alfred*.

In this painting from 1775, the *Alfred* flies the Grand Union flag.

General George Washington led the colonists' fight against the British Army during the Revolutionary War. He used the Grand Union flag in January 1776. The flag flew on Prospect Hill in Somerville, Massachusetts.

without knowing or intending omi
it, for on that day, the day
which gave being to the new
army, (but before the proclama-
tion came to hand) we had
hoisted the Union Flag in com-
pliment to the United Colonies;
but behold! it was received in
Boston as a token of the deep
impression the Speech had made
upon us, and as a signal of sub-
mission, so we *learn*[99] by a per- 99 S
son out of Boston last night. me.
By this time, I presume, they
begin to think it strange that
we have not made a formal sur-
render of our Lines. Admiral
Shuldam is arrived at Boston.
The 55th and *greatest*[100] part, if 10

a copy of a letter Washington wrote about raising the Grand Union flag on Prospect Hill in 1776

The Union Jack on the corner confused British soldiers. They thought Washington was giving up. It was clear America needed a new flag.

portrait of George Washington

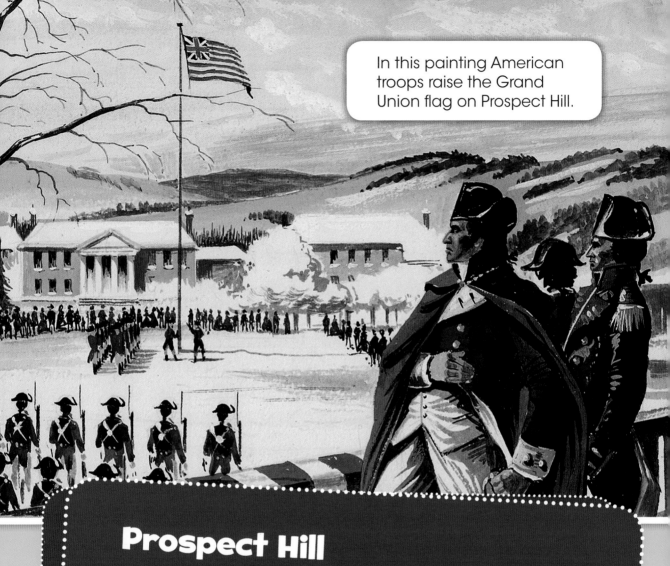

In this painting American troops raise the Grand Union flag on Prospect Hill.

Prospect Hill

Just outside of Boston, Massachusetts, Prospect Hill was once part of a quiet dairy farm. During the Revolutionary War, Continental Army soldiers used the hill as a command center. From 1777 to 1778, the hill was used to hold British Army prisoners.

Who Made the U.S. Flag?

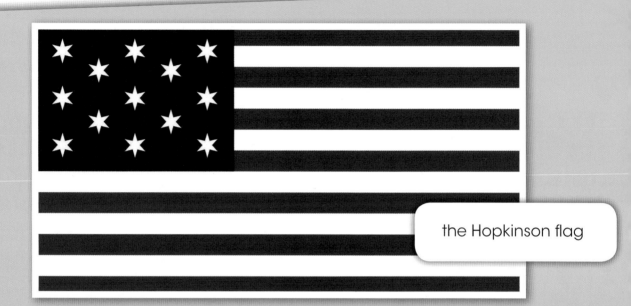

the Hopkinson flag

No one is sure who made the first U.S. flag. Some people believe Francis Hopkinson created the flag. And there may be proof. In 1780 Hopkinson sent a bill to the U.S. Board of Treasury for his work on the U.S. flag. However the bill was never paid.

FACT

Francis Hopkinson was a politician, writer, and artist. He also served as a lawyer and a judge. Hopkinson signed the Declaration of Independence. He also helped design American money.

10

portrait of Francis Hopkinson

Many people believe Betsy Ross made the first flag. Ross was a flagmaker. She made flags for the Pennsylvania Navy. Her grandson, William Canby, said Ross met with George Washington in 1776.

a 1908 portrait of Betsy Ross

FACT

People believe Betsy Ross thought the flag's stars should have five points. This was because five points were easier to cut than six points.

In this 1917 painting, Betsy Ross shows her flag design to George Washington.

Nothing proves Ross made the first flag. Her grandson had no evidence. But he said that he had heard the story from his grandmother many times.

The Flag Act of 1777

The Continental Congress wanted U.S. flags to look the same. They passed the first Flag Act on June 14, 1777.

, Aaron
Efq; 5th,
e County

Court of

r Chan-
ovidence,
of Waſhi-
ounty of
e County

t Tabers

A End of Thames-ſtreet, extending from Street to Street, and has a good well of Water. Inquire of MERIAM JOHNSON, living on the Premiſes.

In CONGRESS, June 14, 1777.
Reſolved,
That the flag of the Thirteen United States be Thirteen Stripes, alternate red and white : That the union be Thirteen Stars white in a blue field, repreſenting a new conſtellation.
CHARLES THOMSON, Secretary.

an article about the Flag Act in the *Newport Mercury* newspaper on May 10, 1783

FACT
The first U.S. flag had just 13 stars.

Continental Congress

The Continental Congress was made up of representatives from all 13 colonies. These members are now known as the founding fathers. These 55 members met to create the Declaration of Independence and the U.S. Constitution.

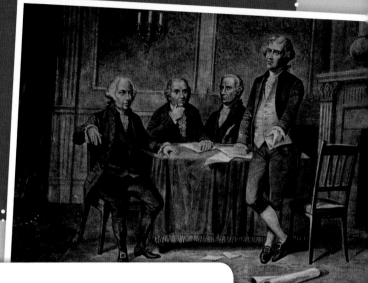

John Adams, Robert Morris, Alexander Hamilton, and Thomas Jefferson were members of the Continental Congress.

Congress decided the U.S. flag should have 13 red and white stripes. These stripes stood for the 13 American colonies that rebelled against Great Britain during the Revolutionary War.

Changing Looks

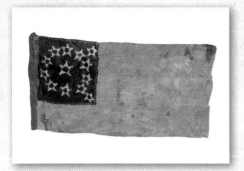

The first Flag Act didn't say how the stars or stripes should appear on the U.S. flag. Early versions of the flag looked very different.

During the Battle of Flamborough Head in 1779, American Navy Captain John Paul Jones flew the Serapis flag. This flag had red and white stripes and four blue stripes. The stars had eight points.

American soldiers carried the Guilford flag in 1781. This flag's stars also had eight points.

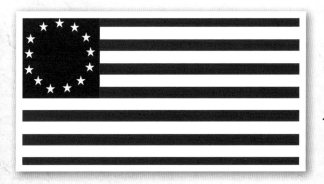

The 13 stars form a circle on the original flag. This design showed each of the 13 colonies was just as important as the next.

More Changes

Vermont and Kentucky became states between 1791 and 1792. Congress wanted to update the flag with two new stars. On January 13, 1794, they passed the Flag Act of 1794 to add them.

a photo from the early 1900s of the U.S. flag with 15 stars and 15 stripes

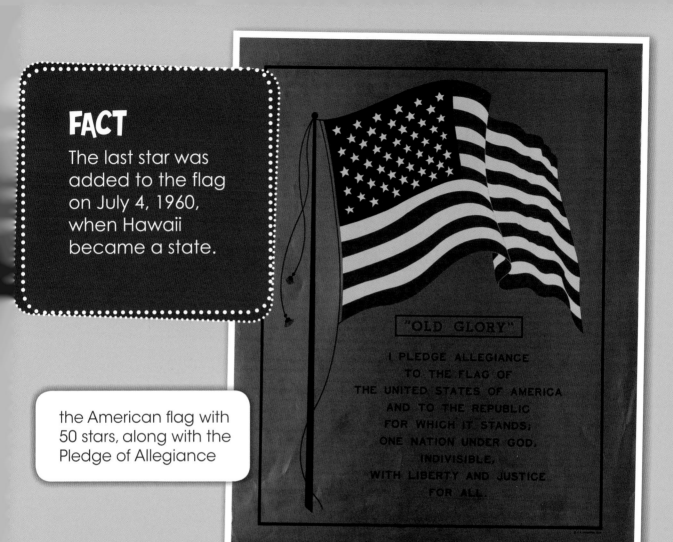

the American flag with 50 stars, along with the Pledge of Allegiance

By 1818 five more states joined the United States. Congress passed a third flag act—the Flag Act of 1818. This act stated that a new star would be added for each new state. Today the U.S. flag has 50 stars.

A Flag with Many Names

The U.S. flag has been called many different names. Some include Old Glory and the Star-Spangled Banner. But what inspired these great names?

In 1824 Captain William Driver's mother gave him a U.S. flag. Driver proudly flew his flag over his ship, the *Charles Doggett*. When the wind caught the flag, he cried out, "There flies Old Glory!"

painting from 1833 of Captain William Driver

"OLD GLORY."   Photo of Original Flag.

During the Civil War (1861–1865), Confederate soldiers tried to take Driver's flag. But he hid it away. Today Driver's flag is at the Smithsonian Museum in Washington, D.C.

portrait of Francis Scott Key in 1825

the Star-Spangled Banner

Francis Scott Key was an American lawyer during the War of 1812 (1812–1815). He boarded a British ship on September 7, 1814. Key was stuck on the ship as the British Army attacked Fort McHenry in Baltimore, Maryland.

Key looked to shore when the fighting was over. The U.S. flag still flew in the air. The fort had not fallen. A surprised Key began writing the poem "Defence of Fort M'Henry." It would later be renamed "The Star-Spangled Banner."

a photo of the opening ceremonies at a major league baseball game in 2008

the first draft of Francis Scott Key's "Defence of Fort M'Henry"

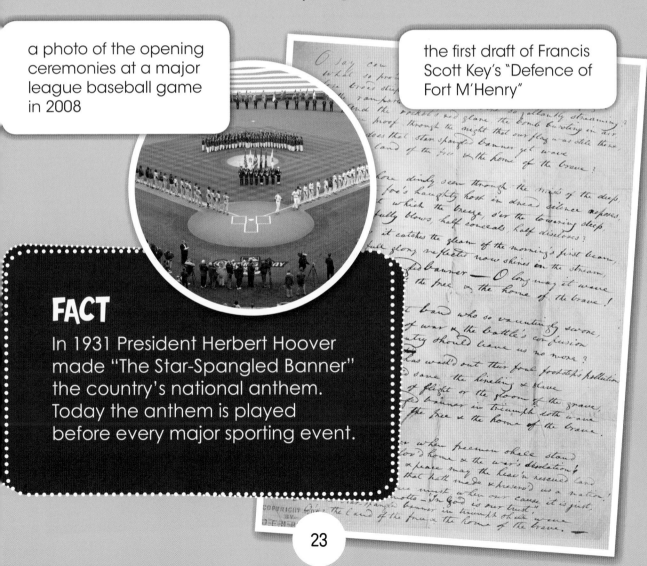

FACT

In 1931 President Herbert Hoover made "The Star-Spangled Banner" the country's national anthem. Today the anthem is played before every major sporting event.

Respecting the Flag

No one knew how to properly display the U.S. flag until 1923. Members of the National Flag Conference gathered on June 14. They created the U.S. Flag Code. The code said when flags should be raised and lowered. The code also said where flags should be flown.

This photo from 2008 shows sailors folding an American flag during a military funeral.

In 1942 President Franklin D. Roosevelt signed the Flag Code into law. However there are no punishments for breaking this law.

President Franklin D. Roosevelt in 1941

The U.S. Flag Today

The U.S. flag remains an important symbol. U.S. flags are flown for special events. We celebrate Flag Day on June 14 each year. Citizens also display the flag on Memorial Day and Veterans Day. The flags remind us of those who fought for our freedom.

a photo of U.S. flags at half mast in New York City on September 11, 2014

Timeline

1775   first U.S. flag called the
        Grand Union is flown

1776   George Washington flies the
        Grand Union on Prospect Hill

1777   first Flag Act passes

1779   the Serapis flag is flown

1781   soldiers
        carry the
        Guilford flag

the Guilford flag

the Flag Act of 1794

1794	the second Flag Act passes
1814	Francis Scott Key writes "The Star-Spangled Banner"
1818	third Flag Act passes
1923	the U.S. Flag Code is signed into law
1960	the last star is added to the U.S. flag when Hawaii becomes a state

Glossary

anthem—a song identified with a group or cause

citizen—a member of a particular country who has the right to live there

colony—an area that has been settled by people from another country and is controlled by that country

confederate—someone involved in the Confederacy before and during the Civil War

Continental Congress—leaders from the 13 original American colonies who made up the government from 1774 to 1789

evidence—information and facts that help prove something or make you believe something is true

glory—something that brings great fame or honor

independence—freedom from the control of other people or things

primary source—an original document

punishment—something negative given to someone for committing a crime or for behaving badly

rebel—to fight against a government or ruler

representative—someone chosen to speak or act for others

symbol—a design or an object that stands for something else

U.S. Congress—the branch of U.S. government that makes laws; Congress is made up of the Senate and the House of Representatives

version—a different or changed form of something

Read More

Harness, Cheryl. *Flags Over America: A Star-Spangled Story.* Chicago: Albert Whitman & Company, 2014.

Monroe, Tyler. *The American Flag.* U.S. Symbols. North Mankato, Minn.: Capstone Press, 2014.

Rustad, Martha E.H. *Why Are There Stripes on the American Flag?* Our American Symbols. Minneapolis: Millbrook Press, 2015.

Internet Sites

FactHound offers a safe, fun way to find Internet sites related to this book. All of the sites on FactHound have been researched by our staff.

Here's all you do:

Visit *www.facthound.com*

Type in this code: 9781491482223

Check out projects, games and lots more at
www.capstonekids.com

Critical Thinking Using the Common Core

1. The U.S. flag is a symbol of freedom and liberty. What does "symbol" mean? (Craft and Structure)

2. Why did the British Army think General Washington was giving up when he waved the Grand Union flag on Prospect Hill? Use the text to help you with your answer. (Key Ideas and Details)

3. Betsy Ross and Francis Hopkinson have been credited with making the first U.S. flag. Imagine if General Washington asked you to design a flag for the new nation. What would it look like? (Integration of Knowledge and Ideas)

Index